TABLE FO CONTESTS

INTRODUCTION

In a single moment, in a single diagnosis, and without any preparation, I became an accidental caregiver almost overnight. Take it from me, the role of caregiving is no laughing matter, period. However, in my case, the empowering strength of unexpected humor became the glue that held my life together as a caregiver for my old school and feisty 71-year old mother.

I hope for this book proves valuable to anyone who's a caregiver, especially those who are new caregivers for an elderly parent. Caregiving is often a thankless job, the effects of which can cause severe strain on all aspects of the caregiver's life. Nevertheless, a caregiver should never lose the ability to laugh. I know, because I almost did.

After experiencing two nervous breakdowns in plain sight of my mother, I had to find a passion for sustaining my spirits during those painful times when I saw my lively and independent mother become vulnerable in a way I have never known. Initially, I was in sheer denial and devastated by the apparent reality that faced me daily. Slowly losing my mother to a sickness was painful.

To compound the issue, I had little to no support from my immediate siblings, who at times seem to be sporadically engaged. My time, my energy, and my thoughts were overwhelmed with providing medical care and emotional attention, filling out forms, and talking to bureaucrats and medical people. However, during the stress of it all, there were unsuspecting moments when mother's unpredictable words or gestures would cause laughter to rip through the atmosphere of tension and change the course of a single moment, sometimes the course of an entire day.

I honestly believe that seeing me laugh without the heaviness of frustration gave my mother an unspoken empowerment of hope. I was afraid of losing her, but in some profound way, she was probably just as scared of losing me. I believe it pained her to see me in despair while committing my life to her well-being 24/7, so she purposely became an ambassador of humor. She made those around her forget her fight with an unwelcome illness and her ever-present struggle to preserve normalcy.

While she deliberately joked for escape, I casually wrote for escape.

Because of my interest in writing, I penned and quickly shared many of those funny episodes on Facebook. The "Mama Peaches" stories became a Facebook hit amongst friends, family, and a growing audience of people we didn't know who, too, were encouraged and enlightened by Mama Peaches or were understanding caregivers in general.

Many of her supporters wanted to meet her, and many inspired me to write a book containing all the Mama Peaches stories. I almost did it. Yes, almost. I don't have all the funny stories recorded in the book. However, many of the most popular stories making the Facebook cut are in this first book of the Mama Peaches' caregiving book reading series. Yes, there are more funny stories and more books to come!

Laughing and being informed help me to be a better caregiver in the long run. So, in addition to the funny stories highlighted in this book, I have included the following resources in the Appendix:

1). A Bonus Chapter right out of the future book called The Mama Peaches Story. Releasing in 2018, the Mama Peaches Story will take each reader behind the funny stories to introduce the life of my mother, who skillfully concealed her sickness to retain her independence and dignity for years. She did it with unspeakable grace and nearly no hint of detection from those who knew her well, including me. It's the story of enduring hope between a caregiver and care-receiver.

2). Nine Critical Caregiver Tips is a must-read section if you are one of the 64 million current providers of care in the USA. Many caregivers, especially the new ones, have no clue what caregiving fully demands and are likely winging it. I certainly was. Reviewing these tips could very well arm you with the knowledge to not only make a difference in someone else's life, but to help you minimize the stress, burn-out, depression, and guilt associated with daily caregiving.

3). Caregiver's Prayer Toolbox offers power and specific prayers to strengthen, support, encourage, and revive those facing the day-to-day challenges of caregiving. The toolbox of prayers is designed to cover nearly every area of the caregiver's life and assignment as a provider of care.

4). Caregiver Resource Guide is included because an estimated 97% of all caregivers receive no prior preparation or education. You don't have to recreate the wheel, because local, state, and federal resources are in place to assist you as a caregiver. And many of these resources are free. Contrary to common belief, knowledge is not power. It's applied knowledge that unleashes the authority to open doors.

The Caregiver Resource Guide is designed to save you valuable time, energy, and money. This guide is just a start as to what is widely available for today. However, I would like to encourage you to continuously seek out resources and updates because the caregiving landscape is constantly changing. Remember, what you don't know could hurt or kill your care-receivers.

In summary, the purpose of this book is to prepare you for perhaps one of the most important roles you will ever play in your lifetime, your loved one's caregiver. Now, let's start our journey together with some Mama Peaches laughter!

[If you are only interested in the Mama Peaches' old-school funny stories, please read sections 1 and 2, as well as the very last page of this book.]

THE MAMA PEACHES' HUMOROUS STORIES

After each story, you will find Caregiver Facts, Scripture References, and Mama Peaches inspired quotes.

- The Caregiver Facts are from the National Alliance for Caregiving (NAC) and AARP Public Policy Institute's report called: Caregiving in the U.S. 2015 – Focused Look at Caregivers of Adults Age 50+.

- All Scripture References are from the King James Bible unless otherwise noted.

- All Mama Peaches-Inspired Quotes are from the upcoming book which includes Mama Peaches' words of old-school wisdom. This book is due for release in 2017.

Chapter 1:   Lights On

Mama Peaches: I don't care what anyone says. I just like a dark house.

Me: Well, you live with me now. And I don't live in the dark. There's light in my house. I don't want my house to be depressing, dark, and gloomy. You got a new address and a new house — this is the lighthouse, and the light represents the presence of God, mama!

Mama Peaches: Huh. *(Rolling her eyes.)*

*[Later during the night. I go to mama's bedroom to
check on her.]*

Me: MAMA, why you got all the lights on in this bedroom?

Mama Peaches: I love the light. I love the presence of God.

Me: *(Smiling.)* Alright. Love you and goodnight. Don't forget to turn off the lights.

[I wake up in the middle of the night and notice nearly ALL of the lights in the house are on. I quickly turn them all off and go to bed. I wake up a few hours later and all the lights are back on again!)

Me: Mama, wake up! Why you turning on all the lights? You didn't have all your lights on at your house like this!

Mama Peaches: Boy, I am trying to sleep.

Me: Why are you turning on all the lights? That's running up my bill!

Mama Peaches: Hell, that's why I kept my house dark with the lights off. I didn't want a high light bill, but you got the presence of the Lord in your HOUSE! So, I figure since He is present in your house, he would help you pay the bill.

Me: Arrrrgh!!!!!!! Good night Ms. Chaney and don't touch my lights.

[End]

Caregiving FACT

A caregiver is an individual who provides care for another person in need—
an aging parent, a spouse, child, or friend. Caregiving can be rewarding, but
it can also be very challenging. Stress from caregiving is common but can
have harmful health effects on both the care provider and care receiver if that
stress is not managed.

Caregiving Healing SCRIPTURE

But his delight is in the law of the Lord; and in his law doth he meditates day
and night. And he shall be like a tree planted by the rivers of water, that
bringeth forth his fruit in his season; his leaf also shall not wither; and
whatsoever he doeth shall prosper.

Psalm 1:2-3

Mama Peaches-Inspired QUOTE

Give without the expectation of receiving and you will never be
disappointed.

Chapter 2:   **The Player**

Me: I know you bought some cigarettes when you went to the gas station.

Mama Peaches: Yeah, I did. It's my money and I am grown.

Me: Yeah, your grown-self ended up in the emergency room a few days ago. You don't need to be playing around with your health.

Mama Peaches: That's my business!

[Hours later.]

Mama Peaches: *(Racing around the house.)* Where's my cigarettes? I know where I had them.

Me: *(Busy typing at the computer.)* Soooo, what's the matter? Your grown-self can't find your cigarettes? Hmm hmmm.

Mama Peaches: *(Looking at me with squinted eyes.)*

Me: Hey, you can't play the player!

[Thirty minutes later.]

Mama Peaches: *(Approaching me and looking me in the face.)* Son, don't claim to be the player until you know all the tricks of the game. Haha.

Me: *(Smelling cigarettes on her breath.)* What the heck?

Mama Peaches: Guess you thought I only had one pack.

Me: Ughhhh! *(Laughing.)*

[End]

Caregiving FACT

An estimated 34.2 million American adults have served as an unpaid caregiver to someone age 50 or older in 2015. On average, 50+ caregivers' recipients are 74.7 years old.

Caregiving Healing SCRIPTURE

BE careful (anxious) for nothing; but in everything by prayer and supplication with thanksgiving let your requests be made known unto God. And the peace of God, which passeth all understanding, shall keep your hearts and minds through Christ Jesus.

Philippians 4:6-7

Mama Peaches-Inspired QUOTE

If you got to fight, you better hit first and you
better hit hard.

Chapter 3:   Missing ID

Me: Have you found your state ID yet?

Mama Peaches: *(Looking in her purse.)* I don't know where that dang thing is. It is usually right in here.

Me: Well, you need to find that ID if you are going to withdraw any money from your bank account this week.

[Hours later.]

Me: Mother, did you find it? Have you found your state ID yet?

Mama Peaches: Yeah, I found one of them.

Me: Huh??? One of them????? Huh? Okay.

[Next day.]

Me: I have been thinking. Let me see that state ID you found yesterday.

Mama Peaches: Gimme a second.

Me: Okay

Mama Peaches: *(Pulls something from her purse and hands it to me.)* Here it is.

Me: This ain't no ID. Dang, mama! This is a Xerox copy of your state ID. It's not the real thing. You can't withdraw money from your account with this piece of paper.

Mama Peaches: They know me at the bank. It doesn't matter.

Me: Lord, now we got to get you a replacement. Jeeeeeeezzzzzuuuusss!

Mama Peaches: *(Mumbling in the background.)* He don't know who I know anyway. He better go ask somebody. I can get my money if I want it. Wish they would try to keep my damn money.

[End]

Caregiving FACT

Caregivers of someone 50+ are 50.3 years old, on average, and most are female (60%). The majority (86%) of 50+ caregivers provide care for a relative, 47% care for a parent or parent-in-law. One in 10 cares for a spouse.

Caregiving Healing SCRIPTURE

BUT they that wait upon the Lord shall renew their strength; they shall mount up with wings as eagles; they shall run, and not be weary; and they shall walk, and not faint.

Isaiah 40:31

Mama Peaches-Inspired QUOTE

When you about to do the right thing, it should not be affected by what you already did, didn't do, or should have done – just do it!

Chapter 4: Beat Down

Mama Peaches: Of all my boys, I liked whipping you the most.

Me: Huh? Where did that come from? Why would you even say something like that?

Mama Peaches: Because you didn't run around the house like your brothers. You just stayed in one place.

Me: What? And that made you like to beat me?

Mama Peaches: Yeah, because I could smoke my cigarette, watch my stories, and whip your butt all at the same time.

Me: You know that was child abuse.

Mama Peaches: That was my house.

Me: It was still wrong.

Mama Peaches: Them butt whippings kept your smart butt out of jail, off the streets, away from drugs, out of the child support courts, AND in school. I was the mama and the daddy. Hell, I did good, boy.

Me: Yes, you did good. Well, thank you.

Mama Peaches: What you say? I didn't hear you.

Me: Stop being funny. You know you heard me.

Mama Peaches: And remember you ain't ever too grown for me to beat that grown butt.

[End]

Caregiving FACT

Most 50+ caregivers say their loved one has a long-term physical condition (63%), while 29% have a memory problem. When 50+ caregivers are asked what they perceive to be the main reason their recipient needs care, the top three problems are "old age" issues (16%), Alzheimer's or dementia (9%), or mobility (7%).

Caregiving Healing SCRIPTURE

CASTING all your care upon him: for he careth for you.

1 Peter 5:7

Mama Peaches-Inspired QUOTE

Give what you can only afford to lose and you will never lose anything you really need.

Chapter 5:   Mama's Boldness

Me: Okay, we didn't celebrate Christmas because you were in the hospital. Now that you are doing better what do you want for New Year?

Mama Peaches: *(Thinking.)* Hmm.

Me: A new appliance, new clothes, flowers?

Mama Peaches: Flowers!!? Ain't nobody want no damn flowers. I ain't dead and it's not Mother's Day. Hell, what am I going to do with some ole flowers?

Me: Excuuuuuse me!

Mama Peaches: Don't ask me WHAT I want! Ask me HOW much I want! Give me money, so I can buy what I wanna buy. That's how you do that, son.

Me: *(Rolling my eyes, laughing, and speaking under my breath.)*

Mama Peaches: You say something boy?

Me: No, ma'am

Mama Peaches: Didn't think so. Now where's my present?

[End]

Caregiving FACT

Nearly half of 50+ caregivers say they did not have a choice in taking on their caregiving role (49%). They have been in their role for an average of 3.7 years, with a quarter providing care for five years or more. Those caring for the care recipients 85 and older have been in their role for 4.6 years.

Caregiving Healing SCRIPTURE

COME unto me, all ye that labor and are heavy laden, and I will give you rest. Take my yoke upon you, and learn of me; for I am meek and lowly in heart: and ye shall find rest unto your souls. For my yoke is easy, and my burden is light.

Matthew 11:28-30

Mama Peaches-Inspired QUOTE

A blessed person lives twice as a child and once as an adult.

Chapter 6:   Smoking Fit

[Mama and I are in the living room. I am working on the computer and mama is watching TV.]

Me: No way!

Mama Peaches: Just let me have one.

Me: No, mother! The doctor doesn't want you smoking.

Mama Peaches: One cigarette is not going to hurt me.

Me: Stop worrying me about the cigarette. You know you have a pacemaker and it's not good for your heart.

Mama Peaches: I got a good heart, son. My heart has been broken, played, cheated, stabbed, rejected, broken, bullied, burned, operated on — and it is still working. Gimme my damn cigarette.

Me: *(Frustrated.)* Here's your cigarette!!!!!!!!!!!!!!!!!!

[Mama takes it with a smile of victory on her face and leaves the room.]

Me: Lord JESUS! You are working my nerves mama, just working my nerves. You've been nagging me all morning long about a cigarette. Heck, you are gonna cause me to smoke and I don't even like the smell of cigarette smoke.

[About 20 minutes later I walk into the living room.]

Me: *(Smelling cigarette smoke.)* What's that smell? Mama, are you smoking in the house? You know I don't allow smoking in here!

Mama Peaches: Oh, I am sorry. Let me get my shoes.

[She walks to the back to her bedroom to get her shoes while still smoking the cigarette.]

Me: Mama, what are you doing? Now you smoking through the house. Put the cigarette out, please!

Mama Peaches: I am looking for my shoes. It won't take long. *(Continues smoking.)* Let me see now. I think they are under the bed in my bedroom.

[She continues to smoke and searches her bedroom for the shoes.]

Me: Ugh!

Mama Peaches: Stop rushing me! That don't make no sense for you to be doing that. I am going as fast as I can. *(Still smoking.)*

Me: *(Pacing back and forth while Mama Peaches continues to smoke and search for her shoes.)*

Mama Peaches: I found them. But let me get some heavier socks on because I don't want to catch a cold. *(Still smoking.)*

Me: Oh, you trying to be funny now.

Mama Peaches: *(Smiling and still smoking.)* You don't want me to get sick now do you?

Me: You trying to play somebody. I see what you're doing.

Mama Peaches: *(Finishing off the cigarette.)* I don't like to be rushed. Here you can take this cigarette butt. I am finished. Ain't no use of me going out in the cold any damn way.

Me: I ain't touching that. You think you slick don't you. *(Breathing deep and walking away.)*

Mama Peaches: *(Speaking quietly under her breath.)* I see I didn't go outside to smoke that cigarette. So, I must be slick. Haha.

[End]

Caregiving FACT

Half of 50+ caregivers report their loved one lives in his or her own home, suggesting that some recipients are aging in place. Those who provide care to the oldest-old are more likely (23%) to report he or she lives in a retirement community, assisted living facility, or a skilled nursing facility.

Caregiving Healing SCRIPTURE

FOR God hath not given us the spirit of fear; but of power, and of love, and of a sound mind.

2 Timothy 1:7

Mama Peaches-Inspired QUOTE

Don't do what everybody else is doing or what everybody expects, do what is right in your heart.

Chapter 7:   Match Maker

Mama Peaches: I want to go home.

Me: I know. But, the doctor said you need to stay with me for now. Remember?

Mama Peaches: It's boring here. This TV is not getting my stories. I want to see the Young and Restless.

Me: I am working on the TV. Please be patient.

Mama Peaches: You sit up here and just work. You don't watch TV. You don't have visitors. You don't get out much. Whew! I can't do it! Boy, you need a girlfriend. You need to start dating again.

Me: Stop meddling.

Mama Peaches: Well, you do. A nice-looking man like you should have a girlfriend. A man has needs.

Me: I am not having this conversation with you.

Mama Peaches: Son, I know you don't want to talk about your last relationship. I understand what happened. She was a damn fool to let you get away. But you really need to have someone special again in your life.

Me: Stop being messy. I got Jesus.

Mama Peaches: Jesus ain't going to crawl up in the bed with you at night, boy.

Me: *(Laughing.)* Mama, stop it!!!!

Mama Peaches: Find another wife or I will for you. Now fix that raggedy-@ss TV and find my damn channel so I can watch my stories, hell!

[End]

Caregiving FACT

On average, caregivers of someone 50+ spend 24.1 hours a week providing care, with 22% providing 41 or more hours of care each week. Three in five are primary caregivers, meaning they are their recipient's sole or primary unpaid caregiver, and only 34% use paid help from aides, housekeepers, or others.

Caregiving Healing SCRIPTURE

HE maketh me to lie down in green pastures: he leadeth me beside the still waters. He restoreth my soul.

Psalm 23:2-3

Mama Peaches-Inspired QUOTE

Your successful tomorrow begins right now.

Chapter 8:   Jack Daniels

Mama Peaches: *(Holding a bottle in her hand.)* I don't want this anymore since I am staying with you for a while.

Me: What's that?

Mama Peaches: This is a bottle of Jack Daniels! I was going to share it with my friends for the New Year but I know you won't let me bring it to your house.

*[Mama Peaches heading in the kitchen while baby
brother Darrell is sitting on the couch.]*

Baby Brother Darrell: Maw, is that a quart of Jack Daniels in your hands? Wait! Where you going with that?

Mama Peaches: *(Agitated.)* I am going to pour it out in the kitchen sink. Your brother *(Referring to me.)* won't let me have it. *(She's now in the kitchen and getting ready to pour the contents of the bottle into the sink.)*

Baby Brother Darrell: *(Jumping up from the couch quickly and rushes into the kitchen.)* Naw maw, gimme that!

Me: *(Standing next to Mama Peaches in the kitchen.)* Go ahead, pour it out!

[Mama Peaches starts pouring the Jack Daniels down the sink before Baby Brother could get to her.]

Baby Brother Darrell: Naw, NAWWWWW...what?

[Mama Peaches continues pouring Jack Daniels with me laughing my butt off.]

Baby Brother Darrell: DAMMMMMM!!!!!

Me: Hahahahahahhah!

Baby Brother Darrell: *(Loud and dramatic.)* Maw, no! Why you do that?? Oh, man. I could have sold $2 shots of that. Hell, naw she just poured out a quart of Jack………. DAMMMM!!!!

Mama Peaches: Hell! If I am not going to drink it, nobody will!

[End]

Caregiving FACT

Six in 10 caregivers assist with medical/nursing tasks, of those 43% did so without any prior training, while 14% report they had some prior training. Fourteen percent of 50+ caregivers who provide medical/nursing tasks find it difficult.

Caregiving Healing SCRIPTURE

I can do all things through Christ which strengthens me.

Philippians 4:13

Mama Peaches-Inspired QUOTE

It is better to have a little respect than a lot of popularity.

Chapter 9: Cheap Card

Me: Here's your mail.

Mama Peaches: Let's see. *(Sorting through her mail.)* Social Security, rent, a bill, and some junk mail. Hmm, what is this? Oh, this must be a late Christmas Card!

Me: Yes, it is. It's from my son, Jessie.

Mama Peaches: Yeah, it's Jessie's handwriting all right. *(Ripping the envelope open.)*

Mama Peaches: *(Pulling out the card and violently shaking it.)* He's cheap. He didn't put nothing *(money)* in here.

Me: Mama, just read the card and be grateful.

Mama Peaches: Hmm, he could have put at least $5 dollars in here. Don't know why that boy is so tight. What does he think I am going to do with more paper?

[End]

Caregiving FACT
Half of 50+ caregivers feel their health is excellent or very good, while 17% say it is fair or poor. One in five reports his or her health has gotten worse because of caring for a loved one.

Caregiving Healing SCRIPTURE
THOU wilt KEEP him in perfect peace, whose mind is stayed on thee: because he trusteth in thee.
Isaiah 26:3

Mama Peaches-Inspired QUOTE
If you dilute and stain the truth, it ends up being a dirty lie.

Chapter 10: Mama's Boyfriend

Me: *(Laughing.)* Don't try to change the subject. Who is he? What is your little nappy-headed boyfriend's name?

Mama Peaches: I ain't telling you. I don't need you doing nothing to my man. Huh, I wish you would. *(Rolling her eyes.)*

Me: Who said I was going to do anything to your crossed-eyed, bow-legged boyfriend? I don't even know the negro.

Mama Peaches: Huh! *(Mama Peaches rolling her eyes).*

Mama Peaches: Well, he got a wife anyway.

Me: You are so wrong for that. Tell me you are joking. You are joking, right? I know you have NEVER been that type of woman, so stop playing.

Mama Peaches: Some things you don't need to know.

Me: Well, I am not all up in your business.

Mama Peaches: Well, you the one who brought the conversation up in the first place. All up in my Kool-Aide and you don't even know the favor. Boy, you better get gone somewhere.

[Mama Peaches laughing and me shaking my head]

[End]

Caregiving FACT

Two out five caregivers of someone 50+ report high levels of emotional stress (38%), while 19% report a high level of physical strain and 17% have experienced a high level of financial strain, because of their caregiving role.

Caregiving Healing SCRIPTURE

And let the peace of God rule in your hearts, to the which also ye are called in one body; and be ye thankful.
Colossians 3:15

Mama Peaches-Inspired QUOTE

Common sense ain't always common with everyone.

Chapter 11: Chicken Wangs

[My brothers, James, Jessie, and Darrell, and I take my mama to a soul food buffet outside Cincinnati, Ohio. Jasmine, Darrell, and Daniel, her grandchildren, are with us also.]

Mama Peaches: *(Standing in the buffet line talking to me and my brothers, James and Jessie).* Fried chicken, turkey, ham, greens, sweet potatoes, mac, and cheese; look at all this good food. You mean to tell me we can eat as much as we want?

Brother James: *(Handing Mama Peaches a plate.)* Yes. Get what you want.

Me: Y'all know what I am going to get.

Mama Peaches and Little Darrell: *(Together)* Fried Chicken Wangs!

Me: You know it. And they better have some hot sauce up in here.

Mama Peaches: If they don't have any hot sauce, I got a small bottle in my purse.

Me: Mama we are not at Cracker Barrel. This is a black-owned establishment and they will definitely have hot sauce.

[Everyone laughing, filling plates with food and sitting down to eat.]

Me: Okay, let me pray so everyone can start to eat. *(Praying over the food.)*

Me: Amen!

Everyone: Amen!

Brother Jessie: Maw, you like the food?

Mama Peaches: This food is so good. I am taking a plate with me.

Me: This a buffet. You can't take food out.

Mama Peaches: You mean we paid all that money and can't take nothing out?

Brother Darrell: You can stay as long as you want and eat as much as you want, but you are not supposed to take any food out.

Mama Peaches: Hell, that don't make any sense. *(Mama Peaches continues eating.)*

[The food and conversation are good. Everyone is now done eating and getting up from the table. Bill gets paid. Everyone heads to the cars. My baby brother Darrell is driving one vehicle with both of his sons (Darrell and Daniel) in his car. James is driving the other with me, my mother, Jessie, and his daughter, Jasmine. Mama Peaches insisted on sitting in the back with Jasmine and Jessie. I sat in the front as James drove.]

Brother James: Maw, what are you smacking on back there?

Mama Peaches: *(No response.)*

Me: *(Looking over the seat at Mama Peaches.)* No, you are not eating some chicken!

Jasmine: Grandma?!! *(Laughing.)* Yes, she is.

Mama Peaches: I wrapped up a few pieces in napkins when nobody was looking. Yeap! Don't tell me I can't have something after I paid my damn money.

Everyone: *(Laughing.)*

[End]

Caregiving FACT

Among working caregivers of someone 50+, six in 10 report their work has been affected by caregiving. Most commonly, 50+ caregivers have gone in late, left early, or taken time off because of caregiving (49%), while 14% have taken a leave of absence, 6% have given up working entirely, and 4% retired early.

Caregiving Healing SCRIPTURE

Greater love hath no man than this, that a man lay down his life for his friends.

John 15:13

Mama Peaches-Inspired QUOTE

If you fall, look up. Where you are looking is
where you are going.

Chapter 12: **Escape Plot**

[In hospital room with my 71-year old mother.]

Me: They are discharging you tomorrow but you have to have constant supervision because of your current health concerns. You will have to leave Knoxville and come back with me to Chattanooga.

Mama Peaches: I don't want to go with you to no Chattanooga. I am going to my apartment right here in Knoxville.

Me: We have to move you out of there, remember? We discussed this already with the doctors. You can't go back there to live by yourself at the moment, so we are moving you in with me until you get better.

Mama Peaches: The hell I can't go back to my apartment.

Me: Well, I am just going to drop you off at the nursing home.

Mama Peaches: Oh, hell naw. Ain't nobody wanna be with them old people. *(Looking mean and rolling her eyes.)*

Me: *(Laughing.)* Lord, Lord, Lord.

[Moments later.]

Mama Peaches: Okay. Chris, what time are we leaving?

Me: Naw, you up to something with your sneaky self. That was far too easy.

Mama Peaches: *(Looking up at the ceiling and smiling.)* I ain't up to nothing.

Me: If you are thinking about running off when we get to the gas station on our way to Chattanooga or when I am in the restroom forget it. I am going to keep your cell phone and your purse.

Mama Peaches: DAMN!!!!!!!

Me: You need to watch your mouth.

Mama Peaches: Hell, you need to watch yours.

Me: I love you anyway.

Mama Peaches: Whatever! You are a trip, boy.

[End]

Caregiving FACT

More than eight in 10 caregivers of someone 50+ say they could use more information or help on caregiving topics. Caregivers most commonly want information about keeping their loved one safe at home (43%) and about managing their own stress (42%). One in four reports it is difficult to get affordable care services in his or her loved one's community.

Caregiving Healing SCRIPTURE

Now the God of hope fill you with all joy and peace in believing, that ye may abound in hope, through the power of the Holy Ghost.

Romans 15:13

Mama Peaches-Inspired QUOTE

A relationship without love is like a car without gas. It ain't going nowhere no matter how long you sit in it.

Chapter 13: Mama's Hair

Mama Peaches: When you going to shape the back of my neck?

Me: I can do it now. Let me get my clippers.

[Holding the clippers in my hands.]

Me: Okay, you want me to just cut it all off.

Mama Peaches: Naw boy. Don't play with me.

Me: You might as well let me to just cut it all off since you always wearing that wig.

Mama Peaches: Naw, I done told you. Go on somewhere. Besides, I might want to put me a ponytail on top of my head and I need my own hair for that.

Me: You need to throw that raggedy wig away.

Mama Peaches: I didn't ask you NOTHINNGGGGG. Just hurry up and cut the back of my neck.

Me: That kitchen back there looking awfully rough, Ms. Chaney.

Mama Peaches: *(Rolling her eyes.)* Keep playing. I done told you already.

[I continue trimming the back of mama's neck.]

Mama Peaches: I want you to take me to Atlanta so I can buy me some hair. I see these girls with all kinds of hair. I am gonna get me some.

Me: Huh? What you know about some Atlanta?

Mama Peaches: Everybody knows you can get some bad hairstyles in Atlanta. I might wanna try something new. You just never know.

Me: Who you trying to look good for?

Mama Peaches: That ain't none of your business.

Me: Well, I better not see him around here in my house.

Mama Peaches: How you know he could have already been here. You ain't my daddy and you can't keep me from creeping.

Me: Okay, keep talking and I will bolt the doors.

Mama Peaches: *(Smiling with a twisted smirk on her face as she's looking at the window.)*

Me: And I will bolt the windows, too.

Mama Peaches: Damn!

[End]

Caregiving FACT

When asked to gauge how helpful several policies might be to their caregiving experience, the most popular proposals relate to hospitals' or facilities' interactions with themselves, the caregivers. Half would like their own name on their recipient's medical chart, 45% would like to require hospitals to demonstrate medical/nursing tasks, and 43% want to be informed about major decisions. Of three policies focused on providing financial support to caregivers, about a third most prefer being paid for some of their care hours, while three in 10 most prefer an income tax credit.

Caregiving Healing SCRIPTURE

Charity (Love) never faileth....
1 Corinthians 13:8

Mama Peaches-Inspired QUOTE

Shutting your mouth is sometimes the best open defense when arguing with a fool.

Chapter 14: Curve Kicker

Mama Peaches: Nobody told you to tell that doctor my business.

Me: He asked you if you smoked and you were just looking up at the ceiling like you didn't hear the man. We both know you heard the question.

Mama: It was my business and I can take as long as I want to answer the question. I didn't ask you to tell him that I smoke.

Me: We are just concerned about your health, mama.

Mama Peaches: I can smoke anytime I want.

Me: This is a hospital and you can't get cigarettes.

Mama Peaches: Oh, your mama can get a cigarette if she wants, trust that. I wish like hell somebody tell me I can't smoke me one. You need to go on somewhere before you get hurt. I ain't playing today, now.

Me: No smoking.

Mama Peaches: If I really wanted to fire one up in here, ain't nobody going to stop me.

Me: You talking crazy now. I am leaving and not coming back.

Mama Peaches: What took you so damn long to get that point? *(Laughing.)* You just in the way and sucking up all my fresh air. Get gone somewhere, boy.

Me: *(Rolling my eyes.)*

[End]

Caregiving FACT

Caregivers of those age 85 or older are more likely to have already made modifications to their loved one's home, and they also show a greater need for information about incontinence and making end-of-life decisions.

Caregiving Healing SCRIPTURE

Peace I leave with you, my peace I give unto you: not as the world giveth, give I unto you. Let not your heart be troubled, neither let it be afraid.

John 14:27

Mama Peaches-Inspired QUOTE

Be better prepared than you really think you need to be.

Chapter 15: Morning Mishap

Mama Peaches: *(In the kitchen yelling at me and my baby brother, Darrell.)* Ain't nobody saying good morning up in here this morning.

Me: *(In the living room with my brother.)* Good morning.

Baby Brother Darrell: Morning, maw.

[BAAANNNNGGGG!!!!!! Hissing sound following the bang.]

Baby Brother Darrell: What the HELL was that???

[Me and baby brother rushing to kitchen.]

Me: Jesus, what in the world?

*[Lots of broken glass and water on the stove top.
Continued hissing sound.]*

Me: *(Looking at Mama Peaches.)* Was that my nice blue glass bowl? What did you do?

Mama Peaches: *(Trying to look innocent.)* I was just trying to boil some water for my coffee.

Baby Brother Darrell: In a damn glass bowl, maw?

Mama Peaches: Well…….

[Me in the background shaking my head.]

[End]

Chapter 16: **Don't Tell**

Me: Dorothy! You know, Dorothy?!? She was in my first-grade class at Hays Elementary in Cincinnati. You remember her?

Mama Peaches: Naw.

Me: Yes, you remember. She was short. Light skinned with long hair. Remember? Pretty girl.

Mama Peaches: I don't remember her. Now, I remember Gina Jackson with the long hair. That gal had some hair.

Me: Dorothy was my first girlfriend! Remember she use to hang around with me, Paris Hill, Karen Taylor Gina Jackson, and Valerie Tony. She used to bully some of the boys. She had little muscles and we would box-fight when we got mad at each other.

Mama Peaches: I didn't know that.

Me: What? That I was boxing Dorothy?

Mama Peaches: Naw, that you had a girlfriend in the first-grade. You show nuff kept that a secret.

Me: I don't tell you everything. *(Sarcastic.)* Hmm, wonder where I got that from?

Mama Peaches: You got a smart ole mouth. I see why she beat your @ss and why you didn't tell me about her.

Me: Whatever, Ms. Chaney!!!!!!

[Mama Peaches and I are laughing.]

[End]

Caregiving FACT

Only half of caregivers report their recipient has made plans for his or her future care, and just 43% have plans for their own future care.

Caregiving Healing SCRIPTURE

The Lord thy God in the midst of thee is mighty; he will save, he will rejoice over thee with joy; he will rest in his love, he will joy over thee with singing. Zephaniah 3:17

Mama Peaches-Inspired QUOTE

What you give provides more satisfaction than what you often get.

Chapter 17: Wearing What?

Me: I will be right back. Going up the street to the store.

Mama Peaches: Well, you didn't ask me if I wanna go.

Me: I mentioned an hour ago, that I was going to the store. All you have to say is I wanna go.

Mama Peaches: Okay, I wanna go.

Me: Ugh, get your clothes mother. Pleeaasssseeee hurry up!

[Me leaning in the doorway waiting impatiently.]

[20 Minutes later.]

Mama Peaches: I am READY!

Me: *(Looking at mother with her coat, shoulder-strapped purse, and wig. Mildly noticed light color pants that I have never seen her wear before, but didn't think twice or take a second look.)*

Me: Let's go!

[We head to the car. I open the passenger door for her. She gets in and puts her seat belt on and I shut the passenger door for her. I get in on the driver's side, buckle up, turn the key and proceed to back out of the driveway - but get another glimpse of mom's pants.]

Me: MAMA, WHAT ARE YOU WEARING????!!!!!!!!!!!!!

Mama Peaches: My long johns.

Me: Lord, Jesus. You are not going with me wearing some long johns in public. (Pulling back into the driveway.)

Mama Peaches: Well, can I wear some of your pants?

Me: I just washed some of your clothes. Let's just go inside and get you some real pants.

[We are in the house. I am bringing mama a pair of her clean pants.]

Mama Peaches: I can't wear them.

Me: Why not?

Mama Peaches: They are wrinkled. Oh no, Ms. Chaney doesn't wear wrinkled clothes out in public.

Me: But you were going to wear some long johns out in public. Lord, gimme the pants I will press them for you.

Mama Peaches: These young girls wear whatever they want to today. As long as my @ss isn't hanging out; and my clothes are clean and look good, I should be able to wear what I want. Hell, I am grown. Hurry up you taking all day, we could have been at the store already.

Me: Arrrrrr!!!!!!!!!!!!!!!!!!!!

[Mama Peaches laughing in the background.]

[End]

Caregiving FACT

While most (62%) caregivers of someone 50+ are white, 16% are Hispanic. More than a third have a high school education or less, just lower than the percentage who have a college degree (36%). Caregivers' median household income of $55,000 compares to the $53,046 for the United States overall.

Caregiving Healing SCRIPTURE

There shall not any man be able to stand before thee all the days of thy life: as I was with Moses, so I will be with thee: I will not fail thee, nor forsake thee.

Joshua 1:5

Mama Peaches-Inspired QUOTE

Don't meet the deadline. Just have the deadline meet you by planning in advance.

Chapter 18: Prime Meat

[Mama Peaches' niece, Rhonda, comes to visit her in the hospital. I am in the room, too.]

Rhonda: *(Hugging Mama Peaches.)* Hey Auntie Peaches!

Mama Peaches: Rhonda, what you doing here?

Rhonda: I come to see how you are doing. Here's a card for you and some flowers.

Mama Peaches: Now you know you didn't have to go through all of that, but thank you.

[Mama Peaches opening the card, shaking it, and then reading it.]

Mama Peaches. Oh, that's sweet. Chris, come over here put these flowers on that window ledge.

Me: I got them. Cuz, I like these flowers.

Rhonda: Thank you.

Mama Peaches: Rhonda, that's a nice outfit you wearing. You always dress so nice. Girl, look at those shoes. I can't wear nothing that high. They cute – but I just can't wear them.

Rhonda: *(Laughing.)* I have had these old things for a while but thank you.

Mama Peaches: Where's your meat, girl?

Rhonda: Huh?

Mama Peaches: Child, your meat. Frank, your man. Your husband. Your meat.

Rhonda: Auntie!

Me: Oh Lord, you got her started. That's your auntie.

Rhonda: That's your mama. She just says whatever is on her mind.

Mama Peaches: Ain't nothing wrong with a girl having some meat. I am still in the meat market, too. I am old, not dead.

Me: Lord, I don't believe she just said that.

Rhonda: Jesus, Auntie you are a trip.

Mama Peaches: You a trip acting like you don't know what I am talking about.

[Everyone laughing.]

[End]

Caregiving FACT

Most caregivers are married or living with a partner, and 28% have a child or grandchild under the age of 18 living in their household. Six in 10 are employed (59%). Most live in an urban or suburban setting. One in 10 has served in the armed forces, and 15% of care recipients have.

Caregiving Healing SCRIPTURE

He giveth power to the faint, and to them that have no might he increaseth strength.

Isaiah 40:29

Mama Peaches-Inspired QUOTE

God gave you two ears to listen twice as much as
you speak.

Chapter 19: **Best Seller**

[I tell Mama Peaches I was writing a book about her. Here's what happens next.]

Mama Peaches: I can write my own damn book. Gimme me a pen and some paper. It's my story and I get to decide what I want people to know. They don't need to know all my business.

[I give Mama Peaches some paper and a pen.
She starts writing.]

Mama Peaches: *(She stops writing and looks at me.)* I want Angela Bassett to play me in the movie.

Me: Well, alright. Who going to play my part?

Mama Peaches: Who said I am putting you in my book?

Me: Yeah, right. I should be in the book, and I should be the co-star of your movie. So, who are you going to ask to play me? Will Smith, Chiwetel Ejiofor, or Blair Underwood.

Mama Peaches: Steven Urkel, boy. *(Laughing.)*

Me: You got jokes. You are so wrong in so many ways *(Laughing.)* I will just play myself. You got to have a title for your book and movie. What are you going to call it?

Mama Peaches: Hot Peaches Not for Sale!

Me: Hot Peaches Not for Sale?!?!!! What the heck does all of that mean?

Mama Peaches: You got to read the book, son. That's after you buy it. Hot Peaches Not for Sale, but my book will be.

Me: LORD have mercy!!! Whatever! You're being cheap if I have to buy one of your books. I gave you a free copy of my first published book and I signed it for you.

Mama Peaches: You got all those degrees and still don't know nothing. You getting on my nerves. Lord, I done told this boy over and over again anything that's worth something, don't give it away. You GAVE me your book! Now, what does that say about your book? *(Laughing.)*

[End]

Caregiving FACT

Certain groups of those providing care to someone 50+ are more likely to report having no other unpaid help, meaning they are their care recipient's only caregiver. This includes those providing care to a spouse (79% with no help), high burden caregivers (52% with no help), and lower-income caregivers (51% vs. 39% with household incomes $50,000 or greater).

Caregiving Healing SCRIPTURE

Finally, brethren, whatsoever things are true, whatsoever things are honest, whatsoever things are just, whatsoever things are pure, whatsoever things are lovely, whatsoever things are of good report; if there be any virtue, and if there be any praise, think on these things. Those things, which ye have both learned, and received, and heard, and seen in me, do: and the God of peace shall be with you.

Philippians 4:8-9

Mama Peaches-Inspired QUOTE

Never risk what you can't afford to lose.

Appendix A: Critical Caregivers Tips

It is unbelievable that one blink of an eye can drastically change the rest of your life. It certainly did for me. My mother's diagnosis of dementia diagnosis with and Alzheimer's-like symptoms was the probable cause of a benign brain tumor, per her doctor. Because my she was cognitively impaired and at risk of harming herself, the doctor recommended 24/7 monitoring. Thus, I willingly became her care provider.

I honestly thought that the benefits of having her at my side always would outweigh any detriments. Why not? I would ensure that her every need would be instantly met. I would provide a healthy environment, healthy meals, administer her medicines, accompany her to doctor's appointments, and watch as she improved. Despite having the best intentions of being her devoted advocate, there was so much I didn't know and no one to guide me.

I simply don't want any caregivers, especially new ones, caring for an elderly parent to endure the mistakes I made. To avoid my pitfalls, here are nine recommended tips for you, rather you are starting or continuing the caregiving journey.

1). Embrace change.

No matter how organized and balanced you may be, your life will critically change from day one. Let go and embrace the change. Although I retired early about a year before my mother's diagnosis, I enjoyed a flexible schedule to do whatever and whenever I pleased. I made the mistake of thinking I could balance my life and my mother's life.

I quickly discovered that I couldn't execute my daily plans as usual. I had to live in my mother's world as opposed to bringing her into my well-balanced world. Like me, you must prepare for the unexpected, every given second, when taking care of your loved one. A quick trip up the street to the store to get a missing ingredient for your prized casserole dish could translate into an unexpected hour of getting your loved one ready. That's Change. The act of your elderly parent pacing the house with the opportunity of walking out the front door into harm's way could quickly spoil any hopes of you sleeping peacefully through the night. That's Change. You become heartbroken beyond pieces the day that your beloved parent doesn't recognize you, but you must continue to push forward to love and regain your parent's trust. That's Change. I can go on and on, but you must embrace the notion that your changing parent will force a change in how you respond to the new and unexpected challenges as an adult-child caregiver.

2). Provide fewer choices.

I can't begin to articulate how frustrated I was at the beginning of my caregiver's plight. My mother, who had always been an independent woman, was suddenly vulnerable in an unfamiliar way. Surprisingly, her ability to make routine and sound decisions diminished quickly. Initially, I thought she was only playing games with me. Eventually, I discover how utterly wrong I was.

One morning, I let mother sleep longer than usual because she had been pacing throughout the previous night. We didn't know it at the time, but she was struggling with sundown syndrome. Sundown syndrome is a term that describes the onset of confusion affecting people with dementia and usually strikes around sunset. After weeks, of waiting, we finally had a much-needed appointment with a new doctor to address mother's disturbing behavior and the sundown syndrome.

Two hours before the appointment I woke her up to eat, take medicine, and get ready for the trip to the doctor's office. Despite my pleading and begging her, mama did not want to see the doctor. With much effort, I convinced her to take a shower. After mama, had showered, she went to her bedroom to get dressed. We were now an hour from the doctor's appointment. Through the closed bedroom door, I continued to check on my mother's progress. Each time I inquired, she chanted, "I am almost ready."

The drive to the doctor's office was about twenty minutes away, and we had only twenty minutes to get there. After that last suspicious "I am almost ready" response, I had no choice but to knock and open my mother's bedroom door. Oh no, she was still in her bathrobe! At that moment, I realized that we were not going to make the doctor's appointment for which we waited weeks to arrive, and it would most likely be some time before we get a rescheduled date.

I was extremely disappointed in my mother for causing us to miss the doctor's appointment. When I calmly asked why she wasn't dressed and ready, my mother just looked straight ahead as though I wasn't there. So, I asked a few more times. Finally, she said she couldn't find anything to wear.

Here's what I learned from my mother's condition and those who are cognitively impaired. Decision-making can be overwhelming. My mother had a closet peppered with outfits for weeks. However, choosing from the countless number of pants, dresses, sweaters, and jackets was too much to think about for her. I should have provided two to three outfits for her to consider. I should have narrowed my mother's clothing options to help her make a quicker decision. Also, when asking mother questions, she often would not respond immediately. Through the thickness of much-controlled frustration, I would repeat the question. What I didn't realize is a cognitively-impaired individual often needs time to process the information.

Ask yourself a question and silently watch the clock for thirty seconds. It will seem like eternality. Well, it can sometimes take longer for your elderly parent to respond because he or she is processing the information at a much slower pace. Learning to provide your elderly parent with fewer choices and exercising more patience will curb the frustration syndrome for both of you.

3). Be prepared to make difficult choices.

Get ready to make some of the most difficult decisions in your life. Making medical, daily activity, financial, and quality of life decisions never cease. Sometimes what your elderly parent wants will be at odds with what you believe is best. The difference in opinion can cause exasperation and resentment. You will never stop making important decisions, and there is no statute of limitations for every decision you make. A change in health, a side effect from a medication, or changes in healthcare insurance can render yesterday's best decisions useless.

4). Don't wait to make necessary plans.

As painful as this may sound, your elderly parent's ability to make rational decisions could get worse over time, that is, if you have not already crossed this bridge. Assuming your parent can make sound decisions, it is an excellent idea to sit down and address end-of-life issues. Discussing a medical directive, a power of attorney to cover both financial and medical decisions, and other decision can be painfully challenging, but necessary. Sit down with a lawyer to figure out what other documents are needed, such as a Will and Living Revocable Trust. Check the resource section of this guide for more information.

5). Be prepared for strained relationships.

Caregiving can cause a severe strain on your relationship with immediate family and friends. Ask me how I know. Fortunate or unfortunately for me, my household consisted of only my mother and me. However, I had three slightly younger brothers who lived in another state. I duly provided them with updates and eventually made desperate appeals for assistance. My brothers initially gave me the verbal support and encouragement to do what was necessary to ensure my mother's health. They offer to be available to help.

I was losing my brother's needed support in the process. There were times when they wouldn't answer my text messages. Hours of waiting for a response would mature into days before I received a reply, that is if I got a response at all. Most shockingly, none of my siblings showed up for mother's critical brain surgery or her recovery period. My brothers gave every possible excuse from a lack of money to not being able to off work because of a new job. I am sorry, but there's nothing in all of Hell that would prevent me from being by my mother's side.

My brothers accused me of snapping and getting sharp with them. Why wouldn't I? They wouldn't respond in a timely matter to my appeals for help. I was left to file claims, complete paperwork, fill prescriptions, speak to insurance adjusters, make doctor visits, and challenge many of the insurance company's decisions. I just always assumed that if anything happened to our mother, everyone would naturally pitch in. However, I was the only one caught up in the day-to-day chaos of advocating for my mother's life.

Here's a lesson I learned the hard way. A caregiver's perspective is, at times, challenged by his or her family members. As a caregiver, you can't always expect family members or close friends to behave or respond in a matter that makes sense to you. Sometimes those that are close to us and our loved one receiving care, are not equipped emotionally, mentally, and spiritually to provide additional support. It wasn't until the moment that I released my brothers that I could move forward with the realization that it was just mother and me.

Releasing my family enabled me to redirect my focus and devote more energy to support my mother. Rather than chasing family members and close friends for help, I began to uncover useful resources in my community, such as the National Caregivers Support Program. Whether new or seasoned, I advise any caregiver to consider joining support groups to build a network for moral support and invaluable guidance.

6). Find passion in the middle of chaos.

You must locate the glue that will hold you together when everything else fails. Find a hobby or a pastime that allows you to escape and become re-energized. For me, my escape was writing. One day, I decided to post one of my mother's funny episodes on Facebook. It was just a small release for me. However, I had no idea what would happen in the coming weeks.

Family, friends, and people I didn't know couldn't wait for each new posting, which I eventually started calling "The Mama Peaches' Stories." When I didn't post, people would ask for them. They loved my mother, and many wanted to meet her. Repeatedly, people were advising me to write a book containing the funny Mama Peaches' stories. But the real bonus including receiving tons of advice and guidance from people who saw through the funny stories and recognized a son caring desperately for his beloved mother. My passion for writing connected me to a community of supporters, many of whom have traveled caregiver's path. I suggest you find an interest that provides a temporary escape to help regain your balance, energy, and sanity.

7). Be prepared for embarrassing and uncomfortable moments.

There will be awkward and uncomfortable situations. I never knew what mother would say or do when in public. In many respects, my love for mom and genuine gratitude that she was alive and reasonably in her healthy mind allowed me never to become ashamed of what she said or did. While others may have become embarrassed or uncomfortable, I couldn't help but stand proudly for the woman who always stood up for me.

There may be episodes that will make you cringe, such as moments related to a loss of modesty and increasing difficulty with bodily functions. Remember during these moments; your reaction can regain your parent's dignity while reinforcing trust. It's never your elderly parent's choice to cause you any embarrassment; rather it's his or her diminishing ability to maintain control.

8). Seek help!

Some people are ashamed to ask for help or believe that they can be the Long Ranger of care. Find community resources and support programs. As I mentioned earlier, I joined the National Family Caregivers Support Program, and it changed my life. Not only was this organization a bridge to other community resources, but the Program's monthly meeting allows me to confidentially share my experience with fellow caregivers whose collective experiences save me time, money, and energy.

One of our support program members is a retired nurse who initially thought there was no need for her to join. Now, she quickly tells people that she was wrong in her initial assessment of not being able to learn from a support group. The retired nurse has now been an active member for years.

There are so many community organizations and resources that will help you with nearly every decision-making opportunity in your life as a caregiver. Need a doctor referral, input about a procedure, or just advice on how to cope every day – you can get these and many more answers. Also, there are specific resources and organizations for specific medical concerns, such as Alzheimer's, dementia, and brain tumors, just to name a few. I recommend having a few connections with local organizations as part of your care network.

9). Treat your adult loved one as an adult.

Caring for an elderly parent is not like caring for another child. Parents had lived a whole life before their adult child caregiver was even born, meaning they are very set in their ways. A toddler in pampers is learning to become an adult someday. However, an aging parent who requires the attention of a caregiver is an individual who is learning to cope with life today. A toddler can learn to reason. However, a cognitively-impaired parent's ability to reason may become compromised. Thus, care is needed to manage medicines, doctor visits, and day-to-day activities.

Unlike a toddler or child, an elderly parent is most likely capable of having an adult conversation with adult feelings. Elderly parents should receive adult respect; despite the behavior they may display.

Appendix B: Bonus Chapter

Enjoy this free sample chapter from the author's future book from the Mama Peaches' caregiving reading series called The Mama Peaches' Story.

All I can say is heads need to roll along with spilled guts after a Rural Metro 911 paramedic's decision placed my mom's health and life in jeopardy not once, but two times in a single evening. Here's the unfortunate and horrifying story leading up to the 911 call on December 22, 2015. It was a distress call neither you nor I will ever forget.

The day before the ambulance call: December 21, 2015, at 1:30 pm.

Sitting in my mother's doctor's office. I realized my mother needed to be seen by a medical professional as soon as possible and this was the earliest appointment I could get. As I explained to her primary physician, Dr. Kelly Baker, Mama Peaches' behavior was growing increasingly abnormal, and she wasn't sleeping at nights.

After a series of routine medical questions for us and administering a short mental perception test, Dr. Baker suggested that Mother may have early symptoms of dementia. My shunned ears and shocked brain tried to process this unexpected revelation. Surely not! My independent and lively mother was diagnosed with dementia? Dementia was always something that happened to someone else, particularly to people much older than my mother.

Right? I felt a scream of denial in the back of my throat as the doctor said additional tests were required after the holidays.

We left the doctor's office with a prescription for Quetiapine, a sleep medicine, a future date for more testing, and a probable cause to explain her recent disoriented behavior. I had lots of unanswered questions dancing in my head and thought this cordial doctor visit was somehow still inconclusive.

I got the prescription filled and headed back to my mother's apartment as fast as I could. I wanted nothing more than to give her the much-needed sleep medicine. When she didn't sleep, I didn't sleep. I had already experienced several nights of tossing and turning while Mama Peaches religiously paced the floors. The doctor suggested starting her off with one twenty-five milligram Quetiapine pill. The doctor advised us that the medicine could be gradually increased to up 200 milligrams. Of course, that night I only gave her the recommended dose and waited anxiously for the results.

Next Day: December 22, 2015

First and foremost, the single pill had no effect whatsoever. Mama Peaches paced the rooms of her apartment all night long. She didn't eat my prepared breakfast and spent the morning, as well as the afternoon, complaining about everything imaginable and being completely irrational. To my dismay, she was going outside in the cold without a coat while leaving her front door wide open and unlocked while talking to random strangers, many of whom were local drug dealers in her neighborhood.

I continuously pleaded for her to let me take her to the emergency room, but Mama stubbornly and adamantly refused. I finally called her primary doctor for reinforcement. The doctor advised me to call 911 immediately and to inform the dispatcher that Mama Peaches needed to go to Parkwest Emergency Room. However, I sincerely feared the loss of my mother's trust if I went against her wishes and called for an ambulance.

I just couldn't take it anymore. Her irresponsible and irrational behavior made it clear. I had no choice.

My mother's well-being and life were at stake. I nervously made the 911 call and explained that my mother's doctor needed her to go to Parkwest Emergency Room. Within twenty minutes of my distress call, my ears were rattled by screaming sirens as the ambulance arrived in the parking lot with three paramedics emerging from the vehicle: a young man, an older man, and a woman. Standing outside her front door, Mama suspiciously watched the paramedics walk up the two flights of steps that led to her second-floor apartments. As the paramedics approached us, they asked if we called the ambulance. I introduced my mother and myself and explained the reason for the call. Meanwhile, mother chanted in the background, "There's nothing wrong with me. I ain't going nowhere."

After the paramedic, had verified my mother's identity by viewing her state ID, I told them that my mother's doctor needs her to go to Parkwest Emergency Room. The spokesperson for the paramedics was a woman named Stupid-lena. We will call her Stupid-lena since she didn't formally give me her name. Stupid-lena? Yeah, that's right, and you will soon find out why. Stupid-lena asked for the name of my mother's doctor. I told her the name of the medical practitioner, Dr. Baker.

(Now pay careful attention to the reminder of our conversation.)

Stupid-lena responded by saying, "Oh, that's Dr. Kelly Baker at Ft. Sanders. So, we will take her to Ft. Sanders."

Wait, didn't I just tell Stupid-lena that my mother's doctor specifically requested the Parkwest Emergency Room. Okay, let me try this once more, I thought.

"Excuse me," I whispered hoarsely. "I just said Parkwest, not Ft. Sanders Emergency Room."

"I know," she said. She continued by telling me that that Ft. Sanders was closer in proximity and my mother's doctor was also located at Ft. Sanders.

Like I didn't know where my mother's doctor office was located. Really, lady?

I gingerly mentioned the doctor's specific request again. However, she continued as if my words had no weight by saying that the Ft. Sanders facilities were just as nice and more convenient. At this point, I am thinking, more convenient for whom?

"We are taking her to Ft. Sanders and she will be all right," Stupid-lena snorted back in a condescending tone.

In the heat of frustration, I narrowed my eyes and fired back, "No, the doctor said to take my mother to Parkwest Emergency Room. We are not here to debate the doctor's decision!"

Stupid-lena and I went back and forth while the other paramedics and my mother watched. Were we really having this conversation while my mother's health was at stake? Stupid-lena was lobbying for her opinion of convenience, while I stood firm based on the doctor's recommendation. Finally, the older male paramedic shouted over our bickering by saying, "We will take Ms. Chaney to Parkwest and not Ft. Sanders."

Relieved that I had an ally and a trusted word, the fragile truce of silence that now lingered in the air was broken as I dimly said, "Okay." But, it took everything I had to pretend that I didn't hear Stupid-lena whisper Ft. Sanders in the background.

Who was she and why was she deliberately defiant? She was the type of person my mother would warn me never to trust. I would guess her to be in her late 40s, five feet seven, about one hundred seventy pounds, not fat and certainly, not thin. Her spotted roots sprouted the truth; she was not a natural blonde. Why was I not surprised? In fact, her hair fell to her shoulders in stiff unruly waves. Stupid-lena had puffy but diminutive facial features proportioned almost perfectly. I labored intensely to see any ounce of redeeming beauty in her. Perhaps it was the bitter cold edge of her insincere attitude, but there was absolutely no indication that I could trust her.

Since my mother recently had a few bad dreams about me dying in a car accident, she did not want me going near any cars let alone driving my car. If you haven't already guessed, she refused to get in the car with me to go anywhere. Mama Peaches finally agreed to go to the emergency room with the paramedics only if I submitted to her terms, which included staying at her apartment and not driving anywhere. Of course, I only agreed to ease her mind and get her to the emergency room. Wouldn't you?

Now, my next move included asking Stupid-lena to give me the address and phone number for Parkwest Emergency Room. With a forced smile, she wrote it down on a piece of paper. Before she joined the two male paramedics who were preparing to escort my mother to the front door, Stupid-lena placed the paper face down on the coffee table.

I decided to quickly examine the piece of paper that was suspiciously turned face down as opposed to being handed directly to me. I looked and immediately noticed that Stupid-lena wrote the address and phone number for Ft. Sanders, not Parkwest! Really?!!

Okay, Stupid-lena was trying my nerves. Not good.

"Didn't we all just agree my mother is going to the Parkwest Emergency Room per her doctor's specific request?" I firmly demanded.

Stupid-lena had the nerve to talk to me like I was a hood-rat without an education as she explained once again why Ft. Sanders was a better option with convenience being the top reason. She had the wrong guy, on the wrong day, at the wrong time! Who was she talking to in such a matter? The truth is, I have more combined degrees and accolades than Stupid-lena had rings on both of her hands. Apparently, she was fooled by my ski cap, dark Old Navy hoodie, and distressed Levi's jeans.

"Who are you to challenge a doctor's order? You take her to the Parkwest Emergency Room," I bellowed at Stupid-lena as I hardened my face. And I certainly didn't struggle to make my voice louder at this point. My mother's health was at risk.

Again, the older male paramedic broke through the intensity and said, "We will take your mother to the Parkwest Emergency Room." A cold breeze of silence again filled the room, as I noticed all three of the paramedics simultaneously sliding on plastic gloves in preparation to touch my mother. My mother isn't a deadly parasite or virus, I thought. As Stupid-lena was securing her gloves, she made a weak attempt to assure me that they would, in fact, take her to Parkwest while apologizing for upsetting me.

Oh, really? A weak and empty apology. She was only spewing meaningless words that dangled uselessly in the air. The two male paramedics continued escorting my mother beyond the doorway and to the two flights of steps that led to the parking lot. My mother constantly looked over her shoulders, making sure that I would honor her request to stay in the apartment and not go near the car.

Stupid-lena lingered slightly behind the others, just outside the doorway. I caught my breath in the back of my throat, swallowed and asked with forced politeness for the address to Parkwest Emergency Room once again. After all, I was putting my mother's well-being and life in the hands of the two male paramedics and Stupid-lena, so it was important to be polite. With a twisted smirk on her face, she had the audacity to claim that she didn't know the address and quickly scurried to catch up with her paramedic crew.

One thousand one, one thousand two, one thousand three. Yes, I was counting to calm my nerves because I really didn't want to say or do anything that would result in the adverse treatment of my mother (or that I would regret for another reason). What an insult to my intelligence that she expected me to simply believe that a paramedic didn't know the address of a major hospital in the city or couldn't quickly retrieve the address.

Why was the lady playing games and toying with my mother's health? Did I look stupid to Stupid-lena? She's a paramedic, and she doesn't know the local address of the hospital she is alleging to take my mother to, nor is she willing to exercise the courtesy of asking the other paramedics for the address. My distrust of Stupid-lena was confirmed! However, I reminded myself that I was reassured twice by the older male paramedic that my mother would, in fact, go to Parkwest.

I couldn't help but wonder if Stupid-lena would have treated us differently if my mom and I were actually on the west side of town. My mama was probably seen as just a poor black lady from the east side of Knoxville. Regardless, Stupid-lena and the two male paramedics were handling my rock, and there was absolutely no excuse for mistreatment. I watched sharply as the threesome robotically escorted her down the steps and towards the ambulance that awaited them in the parking lot.

As soon as the ambulance with my mother cleared the parking lot, I gathered my things, darted to my car and began to make my way to Parkwest Emergency Room. With a considerable amount of nervous struggling, I finally programmed my GPS to guide me to Parkwest since Stupid-lena refused to help. After I had located the address in my GPS, I started up my car, and I was good to go.

Long story short. En route to the Parkwest Hospital, I called the facility's emergency room to let them know that my mother was being transported by the ambulance to their medical facility and that I, her son and caregiver, was on my way in a separate vehicle.

Guess what? Are you sitting down about now? The freaking paramedics deceived me and took my mother to Ft. Sanders overriding the doctor's decision to take her to Parkwest Emergency Room. I was literally and deliberately sent all the way to the other side of the city while the paramedics took my mother to the hospital of Stupid-lena's choice. My mother was alone, in her disoriented state with no one familiar nearby. The paramedics lied. Who does that? I was literally speechless. I know, don't say a word because I know you are thinking what I was thinking. Imagine the conversations I had dancing in my mind.

And taking my mother to the wrong hospital isn't the end of this drama. Remember at the beginning of this chapter; I stated the 911 paramedics' decision placed my mother's health and life in jeopardy not once, but twice in a single evening. Wait until you find out what other thing happened to my mother in the next chapter, both related to her deliberately being taken to the wrong hospital.

You've just finished reading the bonus sample chapter from Christopher-Charles Chaney's forthcoming book called The Mama Peaches' Story. Please visit www.AuthorChristopher.com to stay updated on the development and promotions for other books in the Mama Peaches' caregiving reading series. If you are just reading the Mama Peaches' Old-School Funny Stories and the Bonus Chapter, please go to the last page of this book. Otherwise, continued to the next section.

Appendix C: Prayer Toolbox

Prayer is the Living Word of God spoken from our lips. His Word is alive, operative, energetic, effective, and it is sharper than any two-edged sword. Every time you articulate God's Word, you release everlasting life and Faith into the atmosphere. In fact, all of Heaven recognizes the Word of God when it is spoken from our mouth. When you hold His Word up to Him in prayer, the Lord will not only hear His Covenant Word, but He will see Himself and His Son (John 1:1-5).

These powerful healing prayers are designed to encourage, to strengthen, and to heal you and any loved ones to whom you provide care. Pray continuously with Faith. Then you will get to know Jehovah Rophi more intimately as the Lord who heals you (Exodus 15:26) and strengthens you in every situation Here are eight healing prayers for your use:

1. Prayer for Salvation
2. Prayer for Healing and Health
3. Prayer for Defeating Bad Habits
4. Prayer for Overcoming Emotional Hurts
5. Prayer for Honoring Leaders
6. Prayer and declaration for Binding, Loosening, and
    Breaking
7. Prayer for Declaring God's Lordship
8. Prayer of Adoration and Thanksgiving
9. Caregiver's Declaration/Prayer

1. Prayer of Salvation

Heavenly Father, in the Name of your son Jesus Christ, I repent of every sin in my life and ask that You will forgive me for being disobedient to Your Will and Your Word. I confess my sins right now. You are Faithful and just in every situation. I believe You will forgive me and cleanse me from all unrighteousness. I confess with my mouth that Jesus is Lord over my life. I believe in my heart that You raised Him from the dead. I ask Your Son, Jesus Christ, to come into my heart now.

I welcome the Holy Spirit into my life. I believe I am reborn and I am saved now and always. I now have redemption through the blood of Jesus Christ. All my sins, iniquities, and transgressions have been forgiven according to the riches of His grace. In the Name of Jesus, I pray.

AMEN!

2. Prayer for Healing and Health

Father, in the Name of Jesus, I come boldly before the throne of grace to confess Your Word concerning my health and healing. Your Word states that You will forgive all of my iniquities and heal all of my diseases. You desire, above all things, that I would prosper and be in good health. Therefore, I ask that You forgive me for allowing fear, un-forgiveness, self-rejection, guilt, rebellion, self-hatred, sin, pride, and bitterness to open the door to any sickness or infirmity in my life. I repent and renounce all these things, in the name of Jesus.

I stand confidently on Your Word over my entire body because Your Son was wounded for my transgressions, He died for my sins, He was buried for my iniquities, and the chastisement of my peace was upon Him. With His stripes, I am healed from the top of my head to the soles of my feet. I decree that every cell, every organ, every tissue, and every system in my body is lining up to operate according to Your original purpose. The mountain of infirmity against my body has been uprooted and no longer has residency in my body. I cast out every lingering and hidden spirit of sickness and disease that may be lurking secretly in my body. I render all evil spirits in my body to be ineffective, inoperative, powerless, and dead. I decree and declare that I am completely and totally healed from the crown of my head to the soles of my feet. My entire body lines up with Your Will and operates in the manner in which You created it.

Lord, as I continue to pray and confess Your Word concerning my healing, my light shall break forth in the morning and my health shall spring forth speedily as Your righteousness goes before me. Now Father, as I have spoken Your Word over my life for healing, I receive Your Healing Covenant for my life. I hold fast to my confession of Your Word, and I stand immovable, knowing that health and healing are mines, NOW! In Jesus' Name, I pray.

AMEN!

3. Prayer for Defeating Bad Habits

Father, by Your authority, I decree and declare that I am a new creature. Old things are passed away and all things have become new. The old me was nailed to the Cross with Your Son, Jesus Christ, so that my body might be made dead unto all evil and sinful habits. I was buried with Him in Baptism and I was raised together with Him by the power of the Holy Spirit so that I might live each day and behave in the newness of life.

Your Son redeems and protects my life from every attack. He crowns me with loving kindness and tender mercies. In Him, I live and have my being. I have been delivered from the control and dominion of darkness; I have been transferred into the Kingdom of Light. I have been crucified with Christ. Nevertheless, I live, yet not I, but Christ lives in me.

I am an overcomer. I overcome all evil, temptations, addictions, and strongholds through the power of Jesus Christ. Because Greater is Jesus Christ who lives, abides, and dwells in me, than the enemy who is in the world. Death no longer has power over Jesus and sin has no dominion over me. Bad habits are now under His feet. He is far above principalities, powers, and rulers of the darkness of this world and wicked spirits in high places. I have complete victory.

AMEN!

4. Prayer for Overcoming Emotional Hurts

Heavenly Father, You sent Jesus to heal the brokenhearted. You sent Him to set the captives free. I plead in the name of Jesus that You will grant me complete emotional healing from both the past and current hurts.

Despite my challenges, I receive Your unspeakable joy and everlasting peace, which passes all understanding. Every care, every weight, and every attack I lay down right now and follow you. In You, I have the strength and the knowledge to resist the spirits of anxiety, abuse, anger, envy, depression, bitterness, hopelessness, loneliness, fear, and guilt.

Where the spirit of the Lord is, there is liberty. I am liberated in You. I thank You for mending my broken heart from every hurt today. I no longer have an emotional weight and I walk in the newest of Your marvelous light. And right now, I accept Your unwavering peace, which transcends all emotional wounds and guards my heart and mind. In the Name of Christ Jesus, I pray.

AMEN!

5. Prayer for Binding, Loosening, and Declaring

I have the Keys of the Kingdom, and whatever I bind on Earth is bound in Heaven. Whatever I loose on Earth is loosed in heaven.

I bind, rebuke, and renounce every known and unknown open door for religious spirits and their works of darkness in my life.

I bind, rebuke, and renounce all slandering against the moving of the Holy Spirit in my life.

I bind, rebuke, and renounce every spirit of deception and error in my life.

I bind, rebuke, and deny every stronghold and demonic influence in my life.

I bind, rebuke, and renounce the spirit of deception and hypocrisy in my life.

I bind, rebuke, and renounce all pride, arrogance, and self-righteousness in my life.

I loose the spirit of obedience and truth over, in, and on my life.

I loose the ministering spirits of God over my life.

I loose the spirit of health in my body, mind, and soul.

I loose the powers of Peace, Truth, Love, and Joy into my life.

I loose Wisdom, Knowledge, and Revelations into my life.

I loose Peace over my home, finances, relationships, and possessions.

I loose greater faith over my life.

I loose the Seven Spirits of God into my life.

I break up the fallow ground in my life and decree the Glory of God forevermore.

I break every ungodly soul tie.

I break every ungodly generational tie in my family line.

I break every curse and vow.

I break the weight of guilt and shame.

I break every hex.

I break every spell.

I break the stronghold of un-forgiveness and rejection.

I break every incantation, worldly ritual, and ungodly tradition.

I break every ungodly covenant, agreement, and allegiance.

I decree that I am free!

I declare that I am free!

I decree and I declare that I am Free forevermore!

In the Name of Jesus.

AMEN!

6. Prayer for Honoring Leaders

Father, I pray for all those who have authority: the President, Vice President, elected and appointed officials, spiritual leaders, heads of every household, educators of the youth, and supervisors. I pray for leaders so that I will lead a more quiet and peaceable life in all godliness and all honesty according to your Word. I pray that all leaders and all the people will humble themselves, pray, seek Your face, and turn from their wicked ways so that they will hear from heaven, receive forgiveness for their sins, and witness the healing of the land. May our leaders flow continuously in the Holy Spirit. I pray that the anointing of God is evident in all that they do. May they walk in Divine health all the days of their lives.

I pray that Angels are surrounding them like a mighty shield. May there be a spiritual hedge of protection around the health, finances, marriages, families, and ministries of our leaders. I declare that wisdom, favor, prosperity, and the peace of God are abounding in their lives. Father, give them the desire to study, understand, and follow the principles of Your Word. May they realize that all authority comes from You, not from men and that one day they will stand before You to give an account of their actions while in the earth realm.

I pray that you will rebuke Satan, the father of lies, for his deception that mankind can make decisions without consulting You. I pray that leaders will trust in you with all of their hearts and that they will lean not on their understanding. I pray that they will acknowledge You in every thought and deed. May You continue to direct their paths.

I pray for our Constitution, our military, and political leaders. Bless teachers who teach our children and parents who rear them. Give all leaders wisdom and courage. Father, may You continue to be glorified on the earth and in the church by Jesus Christ forevermore. In the name of the One who holds the entire world in His hands, by the power and authority of the Lord Jesus Christ, I pray.

AMEN!

7. Prayer for Declaring God's Lordship

Father God, I invite You now to be: Lord over my spirit, soul, and body; Lord over my thoughts, imaginations, words, and actions; Lord of my emotions and reactions; Lord over my physical body, which is your temple; Lord over my eye gates, nose gate, ear gates, and mouth gate; Lord over my hands and all that I touch; Lord over my feet and everywhere step; Lord over my sexuality and identity;

Lord over my home, my family, and my relationships; Lord over my finances, my tithes, my offerings, and my possession; Lord over my time, my sleep, my work, and my service for You in the Kingdom of God; Lord over my desires, needs and wants.

You and You alone are my Lord and Master. I declare your mighty Word over my life as I receive Your restoration, love, and strength. I now stand strong in You and the power of Your might. In the Name of Jesus, I thank you.

AMEN!

8. Prayer of Adoration and Thanksgiving

Heavenly Father, I thank You because this is the day that You have made. I will rejoice and be glad in it. I run to Your gates with thanksgiving and I dance in Your courts with praise. I serve You with gladness and recognize that You are The Supreme Lord of everything. From the rising of the sun to the going down of the same, You are the Alpha and the Omega; the first and the last; the author and the finisher of all things. Your ruling scepter of righteousness rules over all principalities, powers, dominions, and might.

Every knee shall bow down and every tongue shall confess Your Lordship. All things consist by You and You consist in all things. Without You, nothing that was made was made. You are the Great I AM who reveals Himself daily. There is nothing that You cannot do and will not do for those who love You for Your namesake. All of Your promises are yes in Christ Jesus because you are a covenant-making, covenant-revealing, and covenant-keeping Lord. Your Word shall never fade or wither away; rather it will perform everything You send it out to accomplish. Your Kingdom is an everlasting Kingdom. Your dominion will endure forever. Men shall speak of Your glory and power for generations to come. You are greater than powerful. As King David said, Your lovingkindness is better than life. I pause right now from everything to honor You, to adore You, and to energize myself in You.

Great is your Faithfulness, my Lord. Your greatness is unsearchable and never-ending. In Your mighty hand is the power to make great and to give strength to all. The greatness of Your steadfast love never ceases. I choose to praise You all the days of my life because of Your worthiness. Your tender mercies are new each and every morning. Your mercy and goodness follow me this day and all the days of my life. Your Eternal Kingdom is the power and the glory forever. In the mighty name of Jesus, I pray.

AMEN!

9. Caregiver's Declaration

I trust in you, my God, with all my heart. I'm not weary of my belief and confession. In all my ways, I acknowledge You. You direct my path. I acknowledge You and Your grace over my life despite what I am feeling or experiencing. Because you first loved me, I command every fiber of my being to surrender in obedience to You.

My voice shalt thou hear in the morning, O Lord; in the morning, will I direct my prayer unto thee and will look up. If I can look up, I can get up from any situation. However, I will be blessed to lie down in peace and my sleep will be sweet – any time of day or night.

I am clothed with God's armor of light and have put off the old man who is corrupt. My mind is renewed and I see my present situation as being in Your mighty and trusting hands. Though I understand it not, I will trust that Your thoughts and Your ways are greater than my own.

I declare that You are the God of my breakthrough. You have visited my house and shall return. I expect an overflow of blessings starting within me. Though I cannot change others, I am empowered by You, God, to choose life, health, and strength. I decree and declare that I have the mind of Christ, the wisdom of God, the sanity of a saint, the spiritual understanding of a true worshipper, and my memory is blessed.

You are my God, who satisfies my mouth with good things so that my youth is renewed like the eagles. In You, I am able to rise above all foolishness, family drama, financial challenges, physical attacks, and emotional assaults. I am what You say I am: A fighter and Heir of Righteousness. I am appointed as a Caregiver in this season. Truth sets me free. I know the truth (belt of truth), believe the truth (shield of the faith), and speak the truth (sword of the Spirit); I stand right before You in truth (breastplate of righteousness); I bring the gospel of peace to my loved ones in truth (shoes of the gospel of peace), and I am saved from all evil in truth (helmet of salvation).

Thank you, My Father, that my life is being rebuilt on a solid rock and no storms of life can make me fall. Violent winds only prepare me to walk in confident in Your mighty strength, anointing, and power.

AMEN!

Appendix D: Caregiver Resources

Administration on Aging

For caregiver support groups, respite providers, and other caregiving services.

Adult Children of Aging Parents

Provides a variety of services that offer information, resources, support and community for adult-children as we care for our aging parents and care for ourselves.

The Alzheimer's Association

The Alzheimer's Association offers just some of the following services; Alzheimer Videos, Care Finder, Caregivers Guides, Caregivers Organization Notebooks, Caregiving Training, Caregiving Resources.

Alzheimer and Dementia Caregiver Center

Provides information and resources to help caregivers as their loved one's journey through the early, middle and late stage development for Alzheimer and Dementia.

American Association of Retired Persons (AARP)

Planning guide with five steps for planning the care of an older family member and tools for each step: Prepare to talk, form your team, assess needs, plan, and act.

American Red Cross

A nine-module family caregiving program is available.

ARCH National Respite Network and Resource Center

ARCH offers planned or emergency care for an adult with special needs to provide temporary relief to family caregivers.

Caregiver Action Network

Resources from the Caregiver Action Network, including a Peer Forum, a Story Sharing platform, the Family Caregiver Tool Box and more.

Caring.com

Caring.com is the leading online destination for family caregivers seeking information and support as they care for aging parents, spouses, and other loved ones. This organization carefully researched and expert-reviewed content includes advice from a team of more than 50 trusted leaders in geriatric medicine, law, finance, housing, and other key areas of healthcare and eldercare.

Caring from a Distance

Information to support long-distance caregivers.

The Dementia Society of America

The Dementia Society of American provides Dementia education, information, and programs for enhancing the lives of those living with Dementia and provide information and support for their caregivers, their care partners, and their communities.

eXtension

The family caregiving resource area of the website includes ask the expert, audio news sections, and articles focused on family caregivers.

Family Caregiver Alliance

Established in 2001 as a program of Family Caregiver Alliance, the National Center on Caregiving (NCC) works to advance the development of high-quality, cost-effective policies and programs for caregivers in every state in the country. Uniting research, public policy, and services, the NCC serves as a central source of information on caregiving and long-term care issues for policy makers, service providers, media, funders and family caregivers throughout the country.

International Longevity Center (ILC)

An international nonprofit organization that focuses on research, policy and education. Formed to educate individuals on how to live longer and better. Log into the site and search for the USA division.

LifeView Resources

Video on caregiving, long-term care, and specific health issues. Some titles are The Educated Caregiver, the Family Guide to Alzheimer's Diseases, and The Family Guide to Long Term Care.

Lotsa Helping Hands

Lotsa Helping Hands is a free caregiving coordination web service that provides a private, group calendar where tasks for which a caregiver needing assistance are posted. Family and friends may visit the site and sign up online to perform a task. The website generates a summary report showing who has volunteered for which tasks and which tasks remain unassigned. The site tracks each task and notification while sending reminder emails to appropriate parties.

MetLife

Information about recognizing the need for care and finding appropriate services for the elderly.

National Caregivers Library

Offers a comprehensive website for caregivers. Provides a variety of forms and templates to help organize family caregivers.

National Family Caregiver Support Program

The National Family Caregiver Support Program (NFCSP), established in 2000, provides grants to States and Territories, based on their share of the population aged 70 and over, to fund a range of supports that assist family and informal caregivers to care for their loved ones at home for if possible.

National Transitions of Care Coalition

NTOCC brings together industry leaders who have created resources to help you better understand transitional challenges and empower you as part of the caregiving team.

Next Step in Care

Next Step in Care provides guides to help family caregivers and health care providers work closely together to plan and implement safe and smooth transitions for chronically or critically ill patients.

Paraprofessional Healthcare Institute (PHI)

This institute promotes the recruitment, training and education curricula for the direct care workforce and polices necessary to support these practices.

Rosalynn Carter Institute for Caregiving

Hosted by Georgia Southwestern State University this institute provides information on caregiver programs, education and training, a community forum, publications, and current events in caregiving for families and professional caregivers.

Senior Life Journey

Senior Life Journey is a not-for-profit organization that desires to offer Creative Music Making experiences to individuals with cognitive and physical disabilities and Hospice Music to those in their last days. Your donations are essential to keep this ministry active.

Wiser Institute for a Secure Retirement (WISER)

Financial Steps for Caregivers: What You Need to Know About Money and Retirement is designed to help you identify financial decisions you may face as a caregiver. The decision to become a caregiver can affect both your short-term and long-term financial security, including your retirement.

The Caregiver Voice (TCV)

The organization serves family caregivers and professionals who work with adults with cognitive impairment or dementia caused by Alzheimer's, stroke, related illnesses, or trauma.

Care Receiver's Discharge Planning

Caregiver Helper, Inc.
Free online service to help families communicate, organize and find resources to support parents or care recipients.

ElderCare Link
Provides a free referral service to community services for older adults.

Eldercare Locator
In partnership with the U.S. Administration of Aging Organization Eldercare Locator provides links to state and local area agencies on aging and community-based organizations that serve older adults and caregivers.

Family Caregiver Alliance
Provides the Family Care Navigator, a comprehensive online guide to help families in all 50 states to locate government, nonprofit, and private caregiver support programs and resources for older or disabled adults in their communities.

National Alliance for Caregiving
In conjunction with Metlife, National Alliance for Caregiving and the United Hospital Fund, Caregiving provides a family caregiver's guide to hospital discharge planning (also available in Spanish) and hospital discharge planning: Helping Family Caregivers. Guides for going through the hospital planning process.

Terra Nova Films
After the Hospital: What's Next? Planning post-discharge care for elderly persons who have been hospitalized.

<u>***Self-Care Resources for Caregivers***</u>

<u>Caregiving</u>
Support and networking available 24/7 from fellow caregivers and professional.

<u>Caring Bridge</u>
Allows users to create free personalized websites that support and connect family members and friends during a critical illness, treatment or recovery.

<u>Family Caregiver Alliance</u>
Services include Caregiving and Depression, Caring for You, and The Caregiving Workshop Archive.

<u>Lots A Helping Hands</u>
An online volunteer coordination service for friends, family, colleagues, and neighbors to assist older adults in need. Offers a private group calendar to organize meal deliveries, rides, and other caregiving tasks for loved one.

<u>National Alliance for Caregiving</u>
Website with information and support for family and professional caregivers.

<u>Rosalynn Carter Institute for Caregiving</u>
The Rosalynn Carter Institute for Caregiving offers telephone learning series. Free sessions over the phone where caregivers can listen to experts on caregiving and again, and they can ask questions.

<u>The Caregiver Voice (TCV)</u>
The organization serves family caregivers and professionals who work with adults with cognitive impairment or dementia caused by Alzheimer's, stroke, related illnesses, or trauma.

American Bar Association (ABA)
In partnership with the Commission on Law and Aging, ABA provides an online guide to finding legal services in each state, including lawyer referral, court information, state laws and legal rights.

Medicare
A government health insurance program for adults age 65 and older, some people under 65 with disabilities, and people with End-Stage Renal Disease My Medicare and Medicare Interactive are secured online services for accessing and managing personal Medicare information.

Wiser Institute for a Secure Retirement (WISER)
Provides financial steps for caregivers. Specific information is available on money management, retirement, and caregiving.

Long-term Care, Advance Directive, and Advance Care Planning

American Association of Retired Persons (AARP)

Provides a guide to long-term care. Topics include: Thinking Ahead; Staying in Your Home; Choosing Where to Live, How Much Will It Cost?

American Bar Association (ABA)

In partnership with the Commission on Law and Aging, ABA provides a toolkit called Advance Directive. This kit provides a variety of self-help worksheets, suggestions, and resources to help in making decisions about end-of-life care.

Center for Practical Bioethics

The organization offers the caring conversation workbook which makes medical wishes known when severely ill or at the end of life occurs.

The Coda Alliance

Offers the Go Wish Game, which is an actual card game that provides an entertaining way to think and talk about what's important to you if you become seriously ill.

Long Term Care

Offers the Own Your Future Planning Kit by the National Clearinghouse for Long Term Care. This kit provides practical steps for planning ahead for long-term care needs.

Long Term Care Living (LTCL)

LTCL offers printable brochures on every aspect of understanding and shopping for long-term care services.